PASSENGERS

PASSENGERS

MICHAEL CRUMMEY

POEMS

ANANSI

Published in Canada in 2022 and the USA in 2022 by House of Anansi Press Inc.
www.houseofanansi.com

House of Anansi Press is committed to protecting our natural environment. This
book is made of material from well-managed FSC®-certified forests, recycled
materials, and other controlled sources.

House of Anansi Press is a Global Certified Accessible™ (GCA by Benetech)
publisher. The ebook version of this book meets stringent accessibility standards
and is available to students and readers with print disabilities.

26 25 24 23 22   1 2 3 4 5

Library and Archives Canada Cataloguing in Publication

Title: Passengers : poems / Michael Crummey.
Names: Crummey, Michael, 1965- author.
Identifiers: Canadiana (print) 20220203792 | Canadiana (ebook) 20220203806 |
ISBN 9781487011253 (softcover) | ISBN 9781487011260 (EPUB)

Classification: LCC PS8555.R84 P37 2022 | DDC C811/.54—dc23

Book design: Alysia Shewchuk

*House of Anansi Press respectfully acknowledges that the land on which we operate is the
Traditional Territory of many Nations, including the Anishinabeg, the Wendat, and the
Haudenosaunee. It is also the Treaty Lands of the Mississaugas of the Credit.*

With the participation of the Government of Canada
Avec la participation du gouvernement du Canada | **Canadä**

*We acknowledge for their financial support of our publishing program the Canada
Council for the Arts, the Ontario Arts Council, and the Government of Canada.*

Printed and bound in Canada

Benjamin

Somewhere else.
Somewhere else.
How these little words ring.
          —Wisława Szymborska

CONTENTS

YOU ARE HERE: A CIRCUMNAVIGATION   1

Tranströmer on Arrival, St. John's International   5

Tranströmer on Signal Hill   9
Tranströmer on the Southside Hills   11
Tranströmer on Water Street   12
Tranströmer on George Street   13
Tranströmer on the Most Easterly Point in North America   14
Tranströmer on the Bell Island Ferry   15
Tranströmer on the Cliffs of Baccalieu   17
Tranströmer on the Hawke Hills and the Isthmus of Avalon   19
Tranströmer on the Dover Fault   21
From the Island, 1860   22
Tranströmer on Fogo Island   23
Tranströmer on Brimstone Head   24
Tranströmer on Change Islands, 1965   26
Black Postcards   27
Tranströmer on the DRL Coachline, Driving West   28
Tranströmer on the Exploits River   29

Tranströmer on Red Indian Lake   33
Tranströmer on the Gaff Topsails   34
Tranströmer on the Tip of the Great Northern Peninsula   35
Tranströmer on Saddle Island, Red Bay, Labrador   37
An Artist in the North   38
Tranströmer on the Labrador Straits, Near L'Anse Amour   40
Tranströmer on the Landwash at Old Ferolle   41

Tranströmer on the Tablelands, Gros Morne National Park   42

Tranströmer on the Blow-Me-Down Brook Trail   43

Tranströmer on the Port au Port Peninsula   44

Traffic   45

Tranströmer on the Friar, 700 Feet above Francois   47

Tranströmer on the Samiajij Miawpukek Reserve   48

Tranströmer on the Burin Peninsula   49

Tranströmer on Mistaken Point   50

Tranströmer on Signal Hill, Again   51

Tranströmer on Departure   53

Translator's Notes   54

THE DARK WOODS   63

Via Heathrow   67

Belfast   69

Warsaw   71

Innsbruck   72

Stockholm   74

Gdańsk   76

Oświęcim   77

Vienna   79

Sarajevo   80

Kraków   81

Frankfurt am Main   83

Graz   84

Bohemia   85

Native Devil 91

Lucifer at Cards 93

The Devil's Cure 94

Devil's Footprint 95

The White Rock on the Black Road 96

Lucifer on George Street 97

White Devil 98

The Black Man, or Red Indians' Devil 99

Lucifer at Sobeys Square 100

Devilskin 101

The Hinges 103

Saviour's Letter 104

Lucifer at Health Sciences Emerg 105

Job's Cove, Conception Bay 106

Lucifer at St. Pat's Mercy Home 107

Transient 108

A Departure 110

Acknowledgements 113

YOU ARE HERE:
A CIRCUMNAVIGATION

Task: to be where I am.
Even when I'm in this solemn and absurd
role: I am still the place
where creation works on itself.
                              —Tomas Tranströmer

Tomas Tranströmer (1931–2015) was a Swedish poet, psychologist, and translator, winner of the 2011 Nobel Prize in Literature. His work explores the wonder and mystery of human consciousness, often using the stark landscape and weather of northern Sweden as a mirror or a foil for his obsessions.

What follows are loose, amateur translations of pieces I imagine Tranströmer might have written had he recently visited the island of Newfoundland and the coast of Labrador. I've tried to remain true to the spirit and tone and to some of the most obvious strategies of Tranströmer's poetry. But it goes without saying that these pieces would in every way be superior in the original Swedish.

TRANSTRÖMER ON ARRIVAL, ST. JOHN'S INTERNATIONAL

1.
Twice our shuddering plane approaches the runway and sheers off
like an animal at full gallop shying from a fence.

The pilot reins out over the Atlantic, proposing a final pass
before diverting to an airport with a milder disposition.

The voice on the intercom could be a school principal
making routine announcements before the morning bell.

Passengers sitting upright at their narrow desks,
facing the empty blackboard.

2.
Crosswinds rock the fuselage, the engines' waterfall surge
floods the cabin. Our feet reach blindly
for the city as it crests beneath us.

A round of applause when the wheels touch down
as for a street magician who has managed
a sleight of hand on his third attempt.

Once the plane comes to a complete and final stop
a bell chimes above our heads
as if the day's lessons are about to begin.

The bridge leans a hooded face out of its stall
to nudge the forward door,
to nuzzle at our pockets as we disembark.

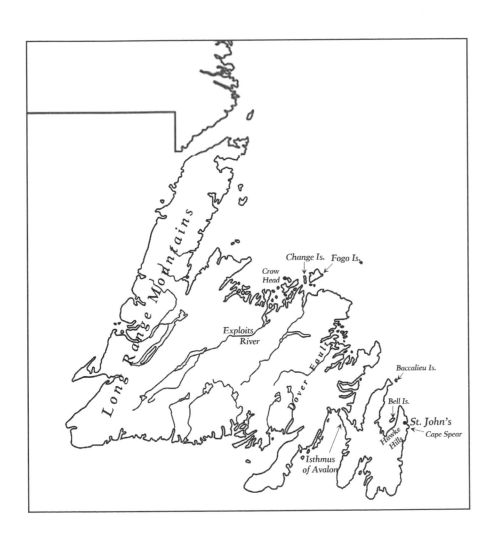

Long Range Mountains

Change Is. Fogo Is.

Crow
Head

Exploits
River

Dover Fault

Baccalieu Is.

Bell Is.

St. John's

Hawke
Hills

Cape Spear

Isthmus
of Avalon

TRANSTRÖMER ON SIGNAL HILL

No tourist escapes cliché.

Some transformative event occurred here
on such-and-such a date.
You lean into period photographs
for the milky-infant scent of the miraculous
as it took its first tentative steps.

The Narrows below Cabot Tower
and the bowl of St. John's harbour
rank with four hundred years of sewage.
Cameras hover like hummingbirds at a feeder
sipping that poisoned nectar.

Your house and its belongings, your mother tongue,
the accumulated effects of a life
sit at anchor overhead,
listening for a word winging from beyond
the ocean you crossed to be here.

A hundred feet of line is as far
as we ever manage to travel
from our selves.
But the world beyond us crowds in,
its walls grow thinner over time.

Through the partitions you can hear
coughing and running water,
the muddy back and forth of conversations

behind the locked doors
of other centuries.

A frail, powdery sound at night
as strangers swarm the far side
of those dividing curtains,
drawn to the glow
of your own little light.

TRANSTRÖMER ON THE SOUTHSIDE HILLS

1.
The Natives are most notable for their absence.
Even their graves are vacant.
The marker erected to explain these circumstances

is playing hide & seek with neighbourhood children
and can't be located. It keeps very still
even after the youngsters go home to their beds,

even when it suspects they've forgotten the game entirely.
It feels surprisingly at ease out of view
as if it was never intended for public display.

2.
On the Heights enormous oil tanks loom over the city
with the malevolent air of prison watchtowers.

At night they are floodlit like casino fountains,
an acid glare that leaves a dark smudge

on the retina when you look away.
A sliver of that desolate light

finds its way into the plaque's hiding place
and purrs at its feet like a cat.

It stands there in silence, arms folded across
the meagre declaration it has to offer the world.

TRANSTRÖMER ON WATER STREET

The city's squalid past occupies the room below your rental.
It has rickety knees and a cantankerous bowel, it never gets enough sleep.
Its grey face is a low-pressure system stalled over the northeast Avalon.
It dreams of flying south to sully a beach in Cuba,
wearing a predatory orphanage as a sunhat.
You nod when passing on the stairs, otherwise
you do your best to ignore the sour hum of its presence.
It resents the pervasive ease of modern life.
When your friends drop by for a drink
it hammers on the ceiling with its cane
to complain about the noise.

TRANSTRÖMER ON GEORGE STREET

Someone has called 911 and the crowd is waiting
for police to arrive, for ambulance sirens
to screw the night's lid that much tighter.

No one knows the specifics of tonight's emergency—
it paces the street in a dark cloak and a plague mask
handing out drink tickets.

Underage girls waver by in cirrus-cloud skirts,
in stilettos that were drunk before they got here.
A terrible mistake pads beside them like a dog on a leash,
they can feel the wet nudge of its snout against their thighs.

Tomorrow night the same generic emergency,
the same dull constellations dancing close to the floor
looking naked and lush as freshly peeled fruit.

It's easy for the young to be happy,
believing their lives are about to begin in earnest.
Watch them stab drunkenly with their keys
trying to find the ignition in the dark.

TRANSTRÖMER ON THE MOST EASTERLY POINT IN NORTH AMERICA

A cordon of signs fixed at intervals
warning visitors not to proceed beyond this point.
Park staff wield bullhorns to harry tourists
intent on dipping their feet,

calling them up from low-lying rocks
where the marbled surf flares and foams at the mouth
and recedes like a nightmare creature
backing into an underground lair.

At night the drowned congregate near the Cape,
stripped of faces by the tides.
How many are out there in the black?
Enough to fill an amphitheatre or the coliseum.

From the wings you can hear rustling
and whispered conversation in that darkened hall.
Like the muted agitation of an audience
as it waits for the stage lights to come up.

TRANSTRÖMER ON THE BELL ISLAND FERRY

The ferry slips from the dock
and the dark ocean jumps to its feet.

Waves clamour at the vessel's skirt like children
accosting tourists as they exit a luxury hotel

hands raised high and a spray of voices
in a foreign tongue.

Bell Island sits in a straight-backed chair across the bay
chinched into its one ill-fitting suit

wearing the fixed expression of the 19th century
awaiting a box camera's flash.

Mine shafts radiate from the island's hub
like the spokes of an enormous wheel.

Pit ponies spent their entire lives
in the crawl space beneath the ocean floor,

stabled underground and shunting ore carts
through the tarry pitch

like the heart pacing its tiny cell,
chafing against the harness.

The mine has been shuttered for generations
but each year that wheel manages

one grinding revolution around
the island's seized axle.

The ferry forges ahead on its impractical heels
slapping at the busy hands of the sea.

TRANSTRÖMER ON THE CLIFFS OF BACCALIEU

A bristling moat of ocean,
the Mackerel cliffs raised like a drawbridge.
The ferment of endless siege—
seabirds in their hand-me-down uniforms
bawling orders from the ramparts.

*

Under every flat stone on the mash
an ants' nest of hoary folk songs,
sightless rhymes tapping their way through
the loam of 18th century carnage—
battlefields and shipwreck and murderous lovers,
good men ruined by the demon drink.

*

The colony's madding crowd huddles on bare rock,
in tenements burrowed into grassy hillsides—
bedlam slums to rival Blake's London
for noise and squalid congestion and filth.

Storm petrels never see the sun
working night shifts in the Atlantic's satanic mills.
Talk of unions and walkouts goes nowhere.
Most of the illiterate masses still think Napoleon
sits on the throne in France.

*

At the island's southern tip
a decommissioned light tower stands at attention—
court-martialed, stripped of rank and duties
and waiting to be dismissed.
An iron key rusted into its lock.

TRANSTRÖMER ON THE HAWKE HILLS
AND THE ISTHMUS OF AVALON

1.

We push off the shoreline into the highway's shallow, brackish river
tacking through a treeless landscape of bedrock and moss.

The Hawke Hills stripped of topsoil by a glacier's grovelling recession,
bowing and scraping while taking leave

of the great halls, the palace courtyards.
Fields of erratics deposited as the ice sheet withdrew

the boxy granite boulders balanced at implausible angles
like figures in a quantum equation.

2.

On the map, the Avalon is reduced to its outline—
a child's crude conception of a starfish

one withered arm demanding the island's attention
with a toddler's grip on the frayed hem of her dress.

There's a single hilltop on the isthmus where
Trinity and Placentia bays are visible north and south

like the mirrored halves of an hourglass
but fog rolls in to claim that seat before we get there.

The details of the world disappear like coins
lost among tissues and lint in a mother's handbag.

What we might make of ourselves is suddenly
too far off to see clearly.

TRANSTRÖMER ON THE DOVER FAULT

1.

Two continents collided along this line.
They exchanged insurance information while
waiting for the police. Adjusters arrived to
assess the damage. Lawyers floated around them
like a boom trying to contain an oil spill.
On the advice of counsel neither party admits fault.

2.

Two continents collided along this line.
One was recently widowed, the other
had been arguing all night with her husband.
It was late, the festivities got out of hand.
Someone turned the lights down low,
someone slipped hallucinogenics into the punchbowl.
Bitterness and blind grief on the dance floor.
They didn't see each other coming.

3.

Two continents collided along this line.
Their curfew came and went as they lay there,
making out in the long grass.
They can still hear voices calling their names
from other time zones. Eventually
they will have to come up for air.

FROM THE ISLAND, 1860

1.

In the back garden she escapes the day's heat
in a wooden tub her mother has filled
with water drawn from the well.

The scathing cold looks straight through her—
a feeling like her skin is made of glass,
like the pale bruise of her self is being erased.

For hours afterward her body shakes with
that terrible sense of nakedness. As if the future
had turned its face toward her and stared.

2.

Every evening he walks the winter miles
from Crow Head to see the woman
he has made up his mind to marry.

One night he loses his way in a storm.
When the weather clears he is wandering
the darkness of another century.

The fresh snow gleams blue in the fields.
Stars settle on his face like moths
drawn to a lamp in a window.

TRANSTRÖMER ON FOGO ISLAND

The island is nursing an unspeakable hangover.
All day it soaks its granite head
in the bleakly medicinal surf.

Your ocean-view B & B is operated by
a *professor emeritus* who never conceded
the History department's lecture hall

trailing guests from room to room
to shell their ignorance with the suicidal tactics,
the cannon-fodder of forgotten battles.

You escape the lilac carpeting to hike the barrens,
to let a cold wind pick the war-dead
from your hair like nits.

The open spaces are almost too raw to take in—
lidless eyes of blackwater flashes,
caribou moss sodden and spongy as a lung.

It's as if the landscape's insides are all on the surface.
Exposed stone cracked by millennia of frost,
fractures that weren't properly set

leaving a permanent hitch in the country's gait.
Even as you walk its naked spine
you can feel the island limping away from you.

TRANSTRÖMER ON BRIMSTONE HEAD

1.
One of the four corners of the flat Earth.
Hunchbacked saint of the lost child.

Two tiers of wooden stairs assisting pilgrims
on the last contested height to the crest

where you meet the cold drizzle halfway as it falls,
where you can just make out

the plunging roar at the lip of things.
A body can stand the bitterness some time

before losing all feeling in the extremities,
in the hopelessly fucked-up heart—

that toy boat coming to grief on the rocks below
as you face the ocean's vanishing point.

Goodbye, vision. Goodbye, little nest of language.
The wind lifts the roof of the world an inch and drops it,

the distressed nails sing like tuning forks.
That note ringing in your chest

when you turn back to Fogo's empty streets,
to the stunted spires of its two white churches.

2.

Grief is a sweater knit by the dead
folded and set on the bedside table while you sleep.

You wear the rough wool like a hair shirt against bare skin
because it was the last thing touched by their hands.

Because the misery keeps them within reach
that much longer.

He is asleep in a bed crowded with brothers, at the centre of that breathing furnace. All night dreaming of burrowing animals at home in dark, enclosed spaces. His mother is first awake, passing by their door and feeling her way downstairs to light the fire. A grate beside the bed sits directly over the kitchen stove. It is like a portal between worlds. The cold clanking of the dampers as she lays the kindling is the sound of a capstan winching an iron chain one link at a time. One by one his brothers rise and dress to join her and he is left alone in the bed's ebbing heat. He does his sums as he lies there. Each number is a step in a long stairway, his hand on the rail as he climbs toward a window on the landing above. Pale daylight through the glass.

A voice from the kitchen interrupts his progress. Then all of their voices are at the grate like prisoners crowding the bars of a cell, each calling his name.

The well sits behind the house. His brothers loop the rope under his shoulders and a busy flock of hands lifts him above the frame, gathering on the line to lower him into the militant chill that radiates from the slate walls. He is wearing all the clothes he owns, his bare fingers gripping a metal cup like a child being sent out to beg for change on a Victorian street corner. He kneels where the groundwater pools just deep enough to be gathered, shouting when the water-bucket is full. Craning to follow the wooden container as it rises an arm-length at a time to the lip.

His brothers' voices are like crows in the highest branches of a tree. The well's frame shows one small square of sky, the night's last star still afloat there.

BLACK POSTCARDS

1.
Wind is the deeper ocean here. We lie at the bottom
of that wild sea, weighting the bed to the floor.
Trees heave their dark crowns against the windows
                of our sunken vessel, wanting in.

2.
In the middle of life it happens that death comes for something
you can't live without. The heart clacks along on its narrow rails.
But beneath your clothes raw stitches mark your grave
                like the X on a map.

Murky aquarium lighting above the seats
and inertia's slow tidal movement from front to back,
from side to side, as the bus accelerates or slows
or hugs the turns on the Trans-Canada Highway.
The island's vacant interior spools by the windows
like a filmstrip looped through a projector—
spruce forest and bog, the lobotomized stare of moose—
but none of it registers where the darkened glass
reflects us back to ourselves, passengers asleep
or riding a line between sleep and the numb attention
that allows whole paragraphs of your book to pass
without a word taking root.
As you nod off a sulphur thought flares—
This is how the dead must travel!
In this invertebrate undersea stillness.
Driving every moment deeper
into the uninhabited.

TRANSTRÖMER ON THE EXPLOITS RIVER

1.
The river divides the journey into halves.

On one side, the traveller dreams of first loves.

On the other, of obsolete technologies—
the hourglass and the abacus,
manual typewriters, pay phones.

On one side, God.

On the other, the idea of God.

To the east are migratory herds of misfortune,
a petting zoo of fossil beds.

To the west the Long Range Mountains descend
like an airport escalator
into America.

2.

Stand in the shallows and the two sides
of the traveller's heart turn to face
one another for the first time.

Circle back to the river
and that wayward creature
is not the same.

The heart is a stranger to itself
each time you step into the current.

Red Bay

L'Anse-Amour

Old Ferolle

← Great Northern Peninsula

Long Range Mountains

The Tablelands

Gaff Topsails

Blow-Me-Down Brook Trail

Red Indian Lake

Port au Port Peninsula

Samiajij Miawpukek

St. John's

Francois

Port aux Basques

Marystown

Burin Peninsula

Mistaken Point

TRANSTRÖMER ON RED INDIAN LAKE

Something has startled the sleeping lake
and it lies half awake in its bed,
in the eddying silt of a dream.

One arm has been trapped all night beneath its weight
and that discomfort leeched into the dream,
leaving its dark stain there.

The lake shifts to free the dead limb,
to dislodge the details wriggling
beneath the bark of consciousness—

A woman stood naked in the shallows.
She was nameless and familiar
like someone recalled

from the earliest days of childhood,
casting a question into deep water
like a hook on a line.

She was reaching for a doorway
the lake hides from the world
by keeping it hidden from itself.

The barbed tip of her voice pricking
in a thousand places as the arm
slowly comes to life.

TRANSTRÖMER ON THE GAFF TOPSAILS

The wind crosses this bare plateau like a medieval army on the march.

Locomotives shorn off the rails, back when there were trains.
Snowdrifts castled on the line stalling progress for days,
dining car furniture sacrificed to keep steam
in the boiler when coal reserves ran low.

The station-stop a circle of wooden shacks for railway workers
and their wives, brought along to face down the gales.
Clean laundry and grace before meals like pegs
to hold their canvas days to the earth.

Looking through the same window morning and evening
to see your stranded heart reflected back to you.
That misshapen pocket watch without hands, without a face.
Pressing it to your ear to hear it tick over the wind's scalding racket.

TRANSTRÖMER ON THE TIP OF THE GREAT NORTHERN PENINSULA

The island is unmoored.
The beach rises imperceptibly above the grey sea
even as it sleeps, face down in its own filth.

The wind rattles and slams like a drawer full of knives.
The few gaunt trees huddle against it like cattle,
stars swimming in their vision—

all day they fight the sensation of falling.

*

Low hillsides submerged in wiry shoals of tuckamore—
dwarf spruce and juniper day-drunk and passed out
on their boarding house mattresses.

There is no beating a path through the disorder.
They've internalized the weather's cruelty
and in their hearts they believe

the weather is their fault.
Their roots are an electrical storm kept
in a box beneath their beds—

They want to live forever. They wish they'd never been born.

*

There is Labrador across the strait.
A woman at a far window

her features impossible to make out
beyond the snowy glint of her teeth.

She has a name other than the one we know,
a name that will never surface on a map.

Our lives are smaller than we imagine.
They have no borders.

TRANSTRÖMER ON SADDLE ISLAND, RED BAY, LABRADOR

Walk past, they are buried.

They stare into the middle distance
like drivers at a perpetual red light,
ignoring the panhandler who taps
his paper cup at their window.

Their graves and the simple music
that buoyed their days have settled,
like sediment in a slow-moving river.

Their native tongue and their vows,
their names and the names
of their lost companions—
the accumulated effects of those lives
like a savings account emptied
one automatic withdrawal at a time.

Walk past, they are buried.

The island lists a little to one side
with the weight of the foreign coins
in its pocket. At night it worries
a thumb across the copper faces,
working the features smooth.

AN ARTIST IN THE NORTH

I, Tomas Tranströmer, move free among men.

I carry a stick to ward off sled dogs nosing
the town's garbage, cocking a leg
to leave their mark on the word "men,"
the word "free."

I have holed myself up here to butt heads with silence.
To lick the enormous empty bowl of it.

Each spring greets the sea ice with a hammer
as dogged as God's heartbeat, each spring
is a broom sweeping that shattered glass
down the ocean's staircase.

I stand on the landing
listening for music that eddies through unlit rooms below
like a lamp carried from window to window
in a darkened house.

The huskies are an orchestra tuning up
in summer's auditorium—
out of harness and pitching sharply toward wilderness.
The stick is how I walk among them
without being set upon and mauled.
The same mute battleground in my heart.

Before I leave I will send out a team of poems
to navigate eternity's bald stare,
the raftered glare of it.
There is no path.
They will make their way across that ice field
without a word from me to direct them.

TRANSTRÖMER ON THE LABRADOR STRAITS, NEAR L'ANSE AMOUR

You are digging for something. Clearing a deposit of stones placed here by hands much the same as your own. You have to rest often, leaning against the rock wall raised by the excavation. A tremor through your limbs that seems to emanate from the stones, as if some blind machinery is rooting in the earth below them. As if a steady stream of traffic is passing several floors beneath your feet. What is down there? Some appalling truth, something hallowed. It calls to you like running water, your heart dipping to the ground like a dowsing rod: here, here, here.

    The pit measures eight meters across, the remains of ceremonial fires blacken its outer edges. The distant headlands pretend not to watch as you off-load that vessel's ballast. They know what's down there. They watched as it was buried in another age, with the same show of indifference. Nearly dark by the time you uncover the body. A young boy in a winding sheet made of bark. He lies face down, a rock slab placed upon his back for reasons beyond your ken. The slab is too large for a single pair of hands to lift. Like grief for a dead child. It is a locked door at the end of a long passageway— you can only kneel beside its weight, forehead pressed to granite. Singing awhile to the silence on the other side.

TRANSTRÖMER ON THE LANDWASH AT OLD FEROLLE

The tide rolls out like a steam train leaving a station. The moon is a silver watch swinging from the conductor's lapel on its chain of stars. An ancient service elevator rattles up from the basement and the rocky shallows step out in their damp scrubs, blinking at the sky, tossing lunch scraps to the gulls.

This is where life first left the ocean with only the clothes on its back, a jewelled family heirloom sewn into the lining of a coat. This is the corridor of power where territories are mapped and divvied up, where the old treaties surrender their swords to new treaties. All negotiations before the wedding receives a blessing, and the negotiations required to keep a marriage afloat, the whispers and backroom deals and weeping, take place here.

Asleep, the mind is a different creature than the mind awake. Primordial thoughts scuttle sideways across its sea floor, oversized pincers raised in surrender or reverence or dread. Twice a day our conscious selves flock here to pick through the litter of our dreams, combing the landwash for stranded shells and devil's purses. For opaque pearls of sea glass.

TRANSTRÖMER ON THE TABLELANDS, GROS MORNE NATIONAL PARK

> End of the line! I ride
> beyond the end of the line.
> —Tranströmer, "Journey"

We are each granted three loves in a lifetime. Tucked into a pocket over your heart, they jockey like sleepers confined to a single bed, like beach stones being milled by the tides.

The distant Tablelands hum with an austere mineral light like a refugee from a fairy tale, a changeling who can read our thoughts, whose single expression is inscrutable. We walk single-file and in silence, as if to avoid spooking the alien presence. As if, like notions of Truth or Beauty, the Tablelands might flicker and slip away as we approach.

The journey is longer than it seems from the road. Further than we can carry what we cherish most in the world and all but a handful have turned back toward the waiting vehicles. Where the climb toward the centre of the Earth begins, the path disappears under stones relinquished by those who came this far and carried on.

TRANSTRÖMER ON THE BLOW-ME-DOWN BROOK TRAIL

At the trailhead, the remains of two poached moose.
Their long faces placed side by side
like plush slippers at the foot of a stair.

The limbs discarded in ditch alder.
You count several times over before confirming
all eight among the camouflage.

The dead world is infinite or nearly so.
It crowds our wake as we travel,
as we climb the steps to our beds,
though by and large it trails us
in anonymous silence.

A cow and her yearling—
their eyes half-closed as if dozing beside a brook
while the irresistible mystery rattles past.

In their dreams they are impossibly light
on their black hooves.
They are practically weightless.

TRANSTRÖMER ON THE PORT AU PORT PENINSULA

The headstones at the back of the hall
are whispering together in French.

The English markers near the front bear
the same names but they have lost the language.

They glare over their shoulders to quiet
the unintelligible murmur in the shadows.

On stage, accordions bloom from the performers' laps
like hydrocephalic foreheads.

They are steam-driven machines with ivory dentures,
they chew with their mouths open

wheezing through a Sunday dinner of jigs & reels.
The players are seated but their feet are in constant motion—

the music is just passing through
and they are trying to catch that train.

A door swings open and the dead stream out
like smoke funnelling through a chimney.

TRAFFIC

The long-distance truck with its trailer pushes through fog.
It has a gannet's astonishing wingspan and sleek carriage,
the same fixed air of purpose as it arrows inland.

Your headlights meet in the dripping gloom.
The big rig's percussive draft slams like a jousting lance,
your car nearly thrown before righting itself and riding on.

A fleet of eighteen-wheelers pass by in twilight,
come from all directions and shuttling north in single-file.
They've spent most of the day foraging at sea,

skimming off the water now to surrender their cargo
to the colony's appetite, to the nestlings' mouths
gaping at the sky like a scarlet field of poppies.

The Long Range Mountains travel beside you
as seabirds accompany moving ships for hours,
a shadowy presence soaring on your port side.

The mountains go to ground before the highway's terminus,
crawling under the ocean's elaborate quilt for a night crossing
to the smoking flats of industry on the mainland.

The dockyard in Port aux Basques. Multiple lanes
of traffic loading in to be ferried across the Gulf.
The vessel like a lesser devil in a medieval vision of hell

swallowing the damned whole: a chain of taillights
cresting the ramp and winking out as they drop
one link at a time into that consuming maw.

TRANSTRÖMER ON THE FRIAR, 700 FEET ABOVE FRANCOIS

1.

You are willing to suffer for the bird's-eye on the crest—
your lungs hooped with brass and slopping at the lip,
each breath winched hand over hand up the sheer.
From this height you watch the fjord elbow its way

to the ocean's varnished dance floor. It loiters at
the entrance, striking the same sullen pose as loners
on the coasts of Norway and Greenland where
nothing human has ever seemed completely at home.

Your coat does its best to keep the wind at bay
but the wind is at every gate, it rattles all the latches at once.
It blows across your heart's open mouth to fetch up
the one wistful note that clay jug was made for.

2.

Below the Friar, the wet roofs of houses glimmer darkly
like pennies at the bottom of a well.

We live with a suspicion we are unwelcome in the world,
that to wish otherwise is futile, but we offer it up regardless.

And making the wish sharpens something in us
it nudges a crack in the door.

A stranger enters the room while you are out
to turn down the bed, to place a single chocolate on each pillow.

TRANSTRÖMER ON THE SAMIAJIJ MIAWPUKEK RESERVE

A rare morning of windless calm. You nod off near the waterline and wake to find yourself surrounded, like the God of Abraham ambushed by evolution. As if life emerged from the ocean as you slept. All this time you have been travelling through Indian country and they have travelled with you—shadows under a false bottom in your shadow's suitcase.

For centuries they held their breath beneath the gene pool's surface glare, silent and stoically patient, as if cast in an old Hollywood Western. A rumour denied even as their footsteps echoed on the circular staircase, climbing toward daylight. They have convened on this shore, a field of fireweed raising their heads for a glimpse of the Atlantic. The sea they look out on is a blue flint under the sun, throwing sparks to the horizon. It burns and burns and is not consumed.

TRANSTRÖMER ON THE BURIN PENINSULA

1.

Stripped of everything not bolted down
and set adrift at the turn of the millennium,
a derelict in the sea lanes until it was leashed
and towed through fog to the Marystown yard
where it sits in dry-dock now, ship-breakers
prying the last century apart a decade at a time,
exposing each deck to the weather's naked spotlight.

We see the future coming and shift our gaze left or right,
the details blurred and listing in our peripheral vision.
It can't help but disillusion us in hindsight.

2.

In a poorly lit shipyard cranny
artificial hearts are being fashioned

from scrap metal, the chambers
jerry-rigged with salvaged piping.

They bleed saltwater and rust.
They will never sink.

Here you are now, at the most remote corner of your life. Your shoes wrapped in disposable cotton boots, the kind worn in laboratories or to avoid contaminating a crime scene. Flat stones jutting in wide, ragged steps above the waves or sloping like a boat launch into the Atlantic. From your knees you can make out the imprint of delicate organisms shaped like spindles and combs preserved in the hardened sediment of volcanic ash— like a suit of armour built to house our earliest, most fragile feelings. It's oddly moving to see the evidence of life in these rocks up close. As if you are leafing through sketches by a gifted friend who shied from her art for the certainties of an office job and died young. What we think of as Time sits like an ocean above the ancient seabed where you kneel engrossed, forgetful. Your days silt down through that weight, draping your stillness in ten thousand layers of soot.

TRANSTRÖMER ON SIGNAL HILL, AGAIN

A crowded escalator of cars ascends the hill
to greet the full moon rising orange over the Atlantic—
a new deck of cards in its shiny cellophane wrapper.

The city shimmers like a crooked casino.
Under the glare of floodlights Cabot Tower leans forward
to give the roulette wheel a spin.

This is when we are most vulnerable, most human.
Before the betting is closed.
While that wheel is in motion.

• *You are here*

TRANSTRÖMER ON DEPARTURE

The airport has mistaken itself for a destination. It insists we take off our coats and shoes and stay awhile. Beneath the surface sheen, a brisk fatalism—everyone is bustling, everyone is melancholy. The restaurants and coffee shops dream of peddling their wares somewhere less contrived. In the meantime they are resigned, grimly efficient.

No one falls in love at an airport despite the banks of high windows, the art on display at entrances, at luggage carousels. Airport conversations are like seat-fillers at an awards show, occupying the gaps that show through our lives as we navigate the dead time before departure. The polished floors gleam like a flight attendant's smile.

The airport is a turnstile. We queue up and pass through, carry-ons nipping at our heels. They sit on their haunches outside security, waiting to roll over. To play dead. Each bag's contents light up on-screen as in a scan of the body's internal organs. But the heart is missing. The heart has already been sent on ahead.

Translator's Notes

Arrival, St. John's International

Many visitors will attest to a similar welcome.

Signal Hill

"Some transformative event": On December 12th, 1901, Guglielmo Marconi received the first wireless transatlantic transmission on Signal Hill, using a kite-borne antenna.

"four hundred years of sewage": St. John's harbour has received the capital's untreated waste since Europeans first settled here in the 1600s. The constricted entrance of the Narrows prevents ocean tides from "flushing" the harbour bowl. A sewage treatment plant has recently been constructed, but it is still illegal to fish in the harbour because of the toxic levels of waste in the water.

The Southside Hills

Shanawdithit, the last known survivor of the Indigenous Beothuk, died of tuberculosis in St. John's in 1829. She was buried in the graveyard of St. Mary the Virgin church, located across the harbour on the city's south side. In 1938, the Royal College of Physicians gave her skull to the Royal College of Surgeons. It was lost in the German Blitz bombing of London during World War II.

Water Street

"predatory orphanage": Mount Cashel, a Catholic orphanage run by the Christian Brothers in St. John's. In the 1980s, the Mount Cashel scandal revealed that many boys living at the orphanage had been physically and sexually abused. The ongoing abuse was covered up by the church, police, and politicians for decades.

George Street

Two blocks in downtown St. John's consisting entirely of bars. The cobbled street is closed to traffic and is often crowded with pedestrians moving from one bar to the next.

"close to the floor": An expression that refers to a tune meant for step-dancing. At community dances, people would request the fiddler or accordion player follow a waltz by playing one "close to the floor."

The Most Easterly Point in North America

Cape Spear, twelve kilometres outside St. John's. The specious "most easterly" claim, which was used to promote the site for decades, conveniently ignored the existence of Greenland. The sea around the Cape is famously unpredictable and unforgiving.

Bell Island Ferry

Bell Island was the site of an iron ore mine which operated from 1895 to 1966. By 1951, mine shafts extended three miles under the ocean floor. Guided mine tours for visitors are now among the few sources of employment on the island.

"chinched": Refers specifically to caulking the seams of a boat, but more generally describes stuffing or packing anything tightly.

The Cliffs of Baccalieu

An island at the tip of Conception Bay's north shore, Baccalieu is one of the largest seabird colonies in North America, home to millions of breeding pairs of murre (referred to locally as turr), razorbills (known as tinkers), puffins, gannets, and storm petrels. The petrels are nocturnal, emerging from their burrows at night to feed on lantern fish and other bioluminescent prey.

"the mash": A stretch of boggy or marshy terrain.

"The Cliffs of Baccalieu" is one of Newfoundland's best-known folk songs, chronicling the near-wreck of a fishing schooner during a storm.

The Dover Fault

A regional geological structure that forms the boundary between rocks once part of North Africa and/or Europe and the rocks that formed the Appalachian Mountains after the continental collision some 410 million years ago.

From the Island, 1860

cf. "From the Island, 1860," from Tranströmer's *For the Living and the Dead* (1995)

Fogo Island

The largest of Newfoundland's offshore islands and one of the oldest named features in European accounts, Fogo Island is home to eleven outport communities. A room at the five-star Fogo Island Inn in Joe Batt's Arm goes for about $2,500 a night. For those of lesser means, many locals operate B & Bs out of their homes.

"flashes": Pools of deep water in a bog

Brimstone Head

"One of the four corners of the flat Earth.": The only documentary evidence for this claim comes from John Robert Colombo's *Canadian Literary Landmarks*: "Fogo Island holds a special place in the mythology of the Flat Earth Society, members of which maintain that the Earth is shaped like a pancake with an Edge or Great Abyss which may be sighted (weather permitting) at the North Pole or off Fogo Island. This at least is the belief of the Flat Earth Society as reconstituted in Fredericton, N.B., in 1973.

(The original Flat Earth Society of Great Britain fell into desuetude some time earlier.)"

"hopelessly fucked-up": The colloquial idiom here is at odds with Tranströmer's customary vocabulary and tone. However, the original Swedish expression is untranslatable and this English phrase comes closest to its spirit and meaning.

Change Islands, 1965

"dampers": The round iron lids placed over the apertures of a wood, coal, or oil stove.

The boy is currently an accountant in St. John's.

Black Postcards

cf. "Black Postcards," from Tranströmer's *The Wild Market Square* (1983)

The DRL Coachline, Driving West

"Driving…/into the uninhabited": European settlement in Newfoundland was driven almost exclusively by prosecution of the cod fishery, and the vast majority of communities in the province are coastal outports. A handful of towns were established inland around mining or forestry ventures but, by and large, the island's expansive interior is currently uninhabited.

The Exploits River

"migratory herds of misfortune": See any work of history on Newfoundland settlement, fishery, or politics.

"a petting zoo of fossil beds": See *Mistaken Point* below.

"The Long Range Mountains descend…into America": The Long Range Mountains on the west coast of Newfoundland disappear into the Atlantic ocean at the southwestern corner of the island. But they are part of the Appalachian mountain system that rises on the east coast of the United States, extending from Maine as far as central Alabama.

Red Indian Lake

Named for the Indigenous Beothuk who were known by European settlers as "Red Indians" for their practice of covering their skin, clothes, tools, and habitations with red ochre. The lake was one of the last refuges of the Beothuk in the years leading up to their extinction. After a debate between local Indigenous leaders, settlers, and government, the name was officially changed to Beothuk Lake in 2021.

The Gaff Topsails

Gaff Topsail is an abandoned railway station on Newfoundland's central plateau. Its name derives from one of a series of granite hills (or tolts) that, from a distance, resemble the topsails of a schooner. The defunct trans-Newfoundland railway line passed through Gaff Topsail, which was notoriously hazardous due to the prevalence of gale-force winds and massive snowdrifts that could close the line for days.

The Tip of the Great Northern Peninsula

"The island is unmoored": During the last Ice Age, much of the low-lying land at the tip of the island was pushed below sea level by the weight of glaciers. The island is still "rebounding" from that compression. The shoreline of a thousand years ago is now hundreds of yards inland.

"tuckamore": Newfoundland term for dwarf spruce and juniper which grow horizontally, rather than vertically, creating a thick, low scrub that is difficult to pick a way through on foot. Their root system can extend up to twelve meters.

Saddle Island, Red Bay, Labrador

From about 1530 to the early 1600s, Red Bay was the centre of a trans-atlantic whaling enterprise carried out by the Basques of northern Spain and southern France. Approximately 140 men who died while prosecuting the whale hunt are buried in a cemetery on Saddle Island in the mouth of the bay.

An Artist in the North

    cf. "An Artist in the North," from Tranströmer's *Bells and Tracks* (1966)

    "raftered": A descriptor for sea ice that has been tilted or piled up by the forces of wind and tide.

The Labrador Straits, Near L'Anse Amour

    Site of the oldest known burial in North America, dated to 7,700 years ago, containing the body of an adolescent wrapped in a shroud of birch bark or animal skin covered with red ochre. After being laid face down in a large pit with the head facing west, a flat stone was set over the corpse's back and the body was covered by a mound of boulders. The Maritime Archaic site was excavated in 1974. The grave was afterwards returned to its original condition, the body reburied as it had been found.

The Landwash at Old Ferolle

    "landwash": Newfoundland term for that part of a shoreline exposed at low tide and submerged at high tide, a liminal territory that is both land and sea.

    Archeological evidence suggests all communities of extended habitation on the island of Newfoundland made use of the harbours and beaches near Old Ferolle over the course of many thousands of years.

    Old Ferolle was renamed Plum Point in 1931 to distinguish the community from New Ferolle.

The Tablelands, Gros Morne National Park

    Gros Morne National Park is often promoted as the Galapagos of world geology. It is one of a handful of places on Earth where the mantle undergirding the planet's crust has been forced aboveground by the movement of tectonic plates. The mantle's richly mineral soil gives it an orange hue. The soil is toxic to plant life and the Tablelands are barren.

The Port au Port Peninsula

    Part of the shifting French Shore of Newfoundland which granted exclusive fishing rights along a portion of the island's coastline to France. The boundaries of the shore altered in each treaty signed after the various wars between the French and English in the eighteenth and nineteenth centuries. The names of those who live on the Port au Port still reflect that heritage though most are now unilingually English.

The Port au Port was the home of legendary Newfoundland composer and fiddler Émile Benoît (1913–1992). There has lately been a renewed interest in the accordion among young players in the area, though most use a modern electric version of the instrument jokingly referred to as "steam powered."

Traffic

cf. "Traffic," from Tranströmer's *Dark Adaptation* (1970)

The majority of Newfoundland's food is imported, most of it arriving via tractor-trailer after a six to eight hour ferry-crossing from the mainland to Port aux Basques on the southwest coast.

"The Long Range Mountains": See note for *The Exploits River*, above.

The Friar, 700 Feet above Francois

The highest point (207 meters or 680 feet) in a circle of sheer cliffs at the end of a half-mile long fjord. The outport of Francois (pronounced Fran-sway) sits at the foot of the cliffs. A rough walking trail will take you to the Friar's summit and back in about three hours.

The Samiajij Miawpukek Reserve

Centred on the community of Conne River, the reserve is home to nearly a thousand Mi'kMaq. Another 2,300 members of the Miawpukek First Nation live off-reserve in other parts of the island. A powwow, drawing people from across Newfoundland, has been held annually since 1996.

Recognizing the large number of families with unacknowledged ties to the Mi'kMaq in Newfoundland, the Government of Canada recently invited applications for membership in the Qalipu Mi'kMaq First Nation, a landless band officially formed by Recognition Order in 2011. More than

100,000 people—fully one-fifth of the province's population—made applications by the 2012 deadline. Over 20,000 have been granted official status.

According to their oral history, the Mi'kMaq took in the last surviving Beothuk in the nineteenth century and that lost tribe became part of their genetic and cultural community. Settler families on the northeast coast of Newfoundland have long believed they have Beothuk ancestors and some of those claims have recently been confirmed by genetic testing.

Mistaken Point

Named for the navigational hazard it poses at the often foggy southeastern tip of the Avalon peninsula, Mistaken Point's tilted and cleaved sequence of mudstones and sandstones are imprinted with fossils of the oldest large, complex life forms found anywhere on Earth. Known as the Ediacaran biota, these creatures lived from 580 to 541 million years ago, when all life was in the sea. The oldest assemblage of these fossils (580 to 560 million years old) is preserved at the Mistaken Point Ecological Reserve. Most of the fossils are representatives of life forms that are now extinct.

THE DARK WOODS

There's only one tune I can play on the accordion,
and even that is a remake of history.
—Lidija Dimkovska

Belfast

Heathrow

Stockholm

Gdansk

Warsaw

Frankfurt

Oswiecim

Brno

Krakow

Innsbruck Vienna

Graz

Sarajevo

Cyprus

VIA HEATHROW

Midpoint of the day-long flight
from an island lately split
between Turks and Greeks
though half the civilized ancients
laid claim to Cyprus as province

or colony or protectorate
at their respective peaks,
each translucent layer
of that halved onion
marked by serial occupation

suggesting the cobbled streets
belong to no one in particular
and I picked up its sour sense
of vertigo like an infection,
a niggling, low-grade fever

that shadowed the visit
and follows at my heels
through Heathrow's expanse
like a last-minute souvenir
stuffed into a carry-on.

Hours of the terminal ring-dance
between connections, pacing aisles
of faux pubs and infernally lit
outlets in the duty-free before
landing among these exiles

in an open-air enclosure,
each wan shade propping a cigarette
and staring blankly into the distance
as if they'd left their hearts behind
or already sent them on ahead.

In the middle of the journey
I came to myself in an alien wood,
in a village that seemed long abandoned,
though lines of smoke ascend
from each grey chimney.

BELFAST

1.

He reported early for his reading, and the librarian
surprised him with a foray into the Belfast phone
book, fingering a column where three variants
of his surname had taken up strategic position
across the city. She said, *By addresses alone*
you can be certain these families are Protestants;
those absent the E are of the Roman persuasion,
and she marked a priest among the latter alliance.
Deployed between the two, a smaller faction
whose nonpartisan spelling and residence
made their loyalties trickier to establish.
He was blindsided by his conscription
into that cross-hatch of sectarian violence.
He hadn't even known the name was Irish.

2.
He read to a select squad of local scribes
taking a bullet for the side, then joined the march
to a pub where the veteran barmaid knew them each
by their usuals—an authority to her presence
suggesting she'd delivered them all and baptized
the lot herself. Paused the roll call when she realized
a stranger occupied the corner seat on her watch
and she demanded his name, his family provenance,
rejecting his disclaimers with a fatal charge:
Your people likely come over here to kill us.
He mustered nerve enough to order a scotch
but she ignored the petition, serving him a stout.
A poet's ashen face warned him not to make a fuss.
He drank the Guinness and kept his proddy gob shut.

WARSAW

The lone corner of the neighbourhood
to survive the war's astonishing indignities
intact. One stark apartment courtyard
shelters a glassed shrine where they prayed
to the Blessed Virgin while Nazis
razed their markets and residential streets.
Latter-day buildings constructed over the refuse
of that biblical onslaught but for these
meagre blocks. A dark brick wall sprayed
with graffiti that our guide translates,
idiomatically, as *I miss you the Jews*.

INNSBRUCK

At her first university post
she taught a Friday evening class

that routinely wandered off the trail
in poetry's sprawling forest—

all night her students shouldered the wheel
as they traced the branching traffic

beneath those tidy lines of print,
talking the moon into morning's furnace.

At the time, eastern Europe was lost
in the dark woods of the Warsaw pact

where writers saddled with a moral compass
risked show trials and internment,

where reading a blacklisted book
was an overtly political act

and poetry had its own small office
in the baroque anthill of dissent

targeted by the surveillance state.
It was an underdog facing long odds,

a charm against a witch's appetite
and they felt a possessive affection for it,

as you would an innocent
abandoned to backcountry wilderness.

Her final undergraduates came of age
after protestors on both sides

managed to topple the Berlin Wall
and slighter concerns briefly took the stage.

The Iron Curtain, the Stasi, the rise
and fall of the Prague Spring: so little

of that grim period survives
it reads like something from a fairy tale.

She never begrudged their lukewarm affair
with poetry in the wake of the Cold War,

it was just the collateral damage
of history losing interest in their lives.

But she missed the raw heat of that fire.

STOCKHOLM

No tourist escapes cliché.

Once you've had all you can stand
of mannequins trussed in the gaudy
togs they wore without apparent regret,
you're in a note-perfect facsimile

of the wood-panelled studio
where those earworms were recorded;
then on a lighted stage singing "Waterloo"
with hologram versions of the band.

An exorbitant additional fee
buys a virtual-reality flight
with simulated rotor chop
to a remote Baltic island

in the Stockholm archipelago,
the foursome's strategic retreat
from the fanatical demand
their confections engendered.

The fag-end of your soul's autonomy
that wishes the tour would stop
is bound and gagged and rendered
senseless while you purchase a seat

for three minutes of Swedish glory
as bright and seductive as their flawless pop.
By touchdown you have surrendered
all notions of escape, of being free.

GDAŃSK

Old Town tourists are mostly German
and geriatric, returning to the city known
as Danzig when they were children
of the master race, each born
to carry the weight of that tin crown
before the war's abrupt revision
purged these streets of every civilian
marked by the Teutonic stain.

They crowd the restaurant
patios and tourist shops, the elegant
boutiques, offering no hint
of what that childhood loss meant,
how it scarred them or to what extent.
Obscene to read it as consent,
but they seem more or less content
to lay eyes on the old haunt

assumed by Poles and Lithuanian
Slavs in their wake, too young then
to process their eviction
and old enough to have outgrown
a parent's scorn for the foreign slant
choking their lost tenement
blocks—consonant on consonant,
the G almost but not quite silent.

OŚWIĘCIM

We followed meekly after our guide's
lightly inflected English explication.

The name, she said, is a Germanized
version of the native *Oświęcim*.

A strict thirty-mile perimeter
between civilians and the barbwire

to keep witnesses to a minimum.
Several tons of shorn human hair

behind a half-wall of glass—
In this room, she said, photos are forbidden.

She herded us to a small green-space
where arrivals judged unfit for labour

were ordered to strip bare on the grass,
guards urging mothers with young children,

the sick and disabled, to mark the place
they set their clothes and belongings,

as if they'd return here to gather
their watches and shirts and stockings

after the obligatory shower.
All day the weather was stifling and clear,

until it was something else altogether.
Between a factory farm of barrack rows

and a crematorium they'd tried to bulldoze
in a panic as the war's buffer

collapsed, a sudden smoking rainfall
forced everyone to run for cover.

It's been years since that aborted tour.
Most of us are running still.

VIENNA

The kind of ostentatious
beauty whose single note rings false.
Everywhere, the ubiquitous
gold leaf of Gustave Klimt's *The Kiss,*
the pointedly religious
spires of a stunning medieval church.
Market street corners busked
by the classically trained who insist
on playing the same goddamn waltz.

SARAJEVO

for Steven

No one dropped in on Sarajevo during the war.
Sarajevo barely slept and rarely left the house

scanning the hills from upstairs windows,
weathering the blockade with black humour

and booze as it waited for the worm to turn.
Or it lay in bed for weeks at a stretch

wishing it had never been born.
Television couldn't get enough of the siege—

a job to keep the factions straight but the tribal
hatred cut through each adulterating particular

like the cleansing stench of bleach.
The snipers are nostalgic for that bloodsport,

they get together on weekends to shoot
Sarajevo in effigy. It makes them feel

they're avenging comrades cut down in court.
It feeds the delusion they campaigned

and killed for something real,
something ordained.

KRAKÓW

> Cities at daybreak are no one's,
> and have no names.
> —Adam Zagajewski

1.
Stitched within the squalid tapestry
now impersonating the squalid 13th century—
a watchman stationed in a cathedral tower
sounding his alarm to the four

cardinal directions, signalling a dust
cloud of Mongol hordes lapping at the city
walls, an arrow to the throat cutting his last
rendition short. That fatal coitus interruptus

repeated every hour on the hour
for crowds of craning tourists
shading their eyes in the market square,
the middle note of the fourth fanfare

awkwardly hacked off, to applause.

2.

I wake to the pealing siren of a woman's voice,
struggle a long stray moment to place
myself—what day? what city?—each detail
winched from the black of a narrow well

as she keens through the Old Town's
streets, a man offering what sounds
like a threat or a drunken appeal
in her wake. She is dragging the chains

of a youthful affair she mistook for love
beneath my hotel window before
the name finally comes to me: *Kraków*.
Home of the apocryphal trumpeter.

FRANKFURT AM MAIN

Travelling for the first time after loss
and at home, more or less,
not living their real lives.

Relying on stock phrases and gestures,
on the generosity of strangers
who speak their language,

they pass through the city's mirage
as they pass through their days—
at one or two removes.

The glassy clutch of high-rises
reminds them of the skyline
in some other metropolis.

They stroll walkways beside the Main
as if scrolling the maze
of maps on a phone,

with the passing notice of tourists.
Feeling not quite lost.
Not quite alone.

GRAZ

These trees took root in the same era as the so-called New World,
that European conceit launched in the late Middle Ages
and still poisoning harbours across the Atlantic.

Victims of the Black Plague interred in this park
though no signs are posted to mark the mass graves
or the subsequent holocausts that forced them to be refilled.

 Anonymous in sin and still spending their paltry wages,
each spring the buried legions leech into the heart-shaped leaves.
The locals lounging, oblivious, in that pestilential shade.

BOHEMIA

for Zuzana and David

The young couple assigned to shepherd
my time settled on a pub celebrated

for simple country dishes prepared
and presented in the custom of tribal Slavs

who occupied the Brno basin, making no effort
to sugar-coat the sacrifice at the heart

of a meal: hard cheese and smoked meat,
a main of pig knuckles and bread

on a broad charcuterie board that served
as our table's one communal plate.

This was ages ago, after a day in the Punkva Caves—
black lagoons and wet slag and soaring stone flues

that could stand in as the muse
for our least palatable notions of God.

Rock caverns vaulted like cathedral naves.
Angels and church spires appearing in a stalagmite

and spotlit like the martyred wooden statues
on display in devotional altars, in grottos,

so true to life they look hand-carved.
Above it all, a stagnant silence

untouched by the commotion created
by our little pilgrimage through the void.

Even after we left that dead-of-night
I was absorbed by a stony reverence,

a cloistered medieval sense
of awe one step removed from dread.

It wasn't until we sat to our food
that I took in how beautiful they were, my escorts,

in love and alive with that heat, elevated
by their innocent appetite

for the world taking shape just ahead—
kids, a home, the prevailing creature comforts.

A garden of modest earthly delight
that each passing year feels closer to sacred.

DEVILSKIN

...in order really to suffer, one has to be faithful.
—Zbigniew Herbert

C.S.Nicolo

RANCIA

R A N C I A

Cap Breton, è
Angoul
P. de Lequier
P. de S.
Germain
Quarti
P.de S.
P. Sant
Antonio
Porto de
Bret
P. de
Carpunt
C.Charles
C.Sable
C.des Chasteaux

PASSAGE DU NORD, ò GOLFE DES CHASTEAUX

FO DI S LUIGI

Grand Bive
aux Balenes

O Bell Isle

C. de Grat, ò
de Grace
Isle S.t Iulien

L' Is. di Terra Nuoua fu scoperta
da Gio. Cabota Veneto. con Se-
bastiano suo Figliuolo nel 1596
li 24. Giugno. a hore 10. per ordi-
ne d'Henrico VII Rè d'Inghilterra
che la chiamò de Baccallaos per
l'abbondanza di questo Pesce

I D I

Saint
Paul

C.de Ra
C.de Ray
C.è Bouteo
C. Aguzzo

Ide Monte
La Grande
Ance

TERRA

C.Rouge, ò
C.Rosso

Baye
d'Orge

Baye
Blanches

Pointe des
Isles de Frere
Louis

Golfa di

I des Oyseaux,
ò degli Vecelli
Parrillon
Frelay
Forelland
Isles de
Frere Louis

NUOVA

detta dagli Inglesi

Baia di S. Giorgio

Coste non ben
ancora ben conosciuta

I. di S.
Giorgio

NEW

FOUN LAND

Port de Bone
Veue

Broitca

Dos Patos

De Graca
Trinita

R S Iuan
Port S.Iuan

C.de Bonne ueue, ò
di Buona ueduta

I. des Molues

Baia della Concetione
detta dagli Inglesi
the Bay off Trintle

C. Saint Francois, ò
S. Francesco et
Enseada Grande

C. de Erphera, ò
de S. Fredage
I. de Galeotas
I. de Columbrina
I. de Ferro
Abra de Brigas
Ferrland
Lau Forte
Roignause

Les
Nuquelet

C.d'Anguille

I.aux Oyseaux,
de gli Vecelli
C. de Raye
Laye

Baye de
Claire
Ance
Las Vierges
Grand Riuiere
de Isles

Baye des Esprit, ò
del Spirito Spto.

Cap. de l'Arne
Chappau Rouge
Isola Marie
Culenta

Baye
Plaisance
Baye
Trapecca

C. d'Anguille

Les Isles S. Pierre

C. de Raz

70 72 60 50 60 60

LE GRAN

BANCO DI
detto dag
MAINE

Banc Vert, ò
Banco Verde

Banc aux Balenes, ò
Banco della Balene

S LORENZO I

45

NATIVE DEVIL

after Zbigniew Herbert

1.

He arrived a stowaway on a wooden ship at the tail end of the Middle Ages.
A frigid fortnight in the bilge, alternately puking and moaning. Christ, he
hated the ocean. Its featureless breadth, its mercurial savagery. How it
inspired the staunchest apostate to faith. Every sailor ends up on his knees
eventually, praying for deliverance.

The country he landed in seemed little more than a breeding ground for
blackflies. An idiot wind, granite half-cloaked in a ragged hair-shirt of
spruce.

It was love at first sight.

2.

During those early years he felt strangely at sea. The fishermen lacked the
time and lumber to raise a chapel, most of his work was done for him. He
wandered the coastline, looking for fallen angels in sea-caves, in drokes of
straggly evergreens. He stumbled on the doomed Beothuk by accident. They
sat immobile when he approached, as if their stillness made them invisible
to the world. They refused to meet his eye. He didn't know the rules of the
game, he grew bored trying to wait them out.

Now and then he encountered an itinerant priest travelling between
outports and they walked together awhile, comparing scars, reminiscing
about the old countries.

3.

Latterly he spends his days panhandling, smoking discarded cigarette butts,
awaiting the Second Coming. He drinks himself senseless in dank

bars, railing against the internet, another ocean he despises. Every abomination reduced to cliché by numbing repetition.

He walks residential streets after dark, leering in at windows. Catching youngsters unawares, baring his crooked teeth to give them a good fright. He spends the small hours of the night in graveyards, bedding down among the marble headstones. Drifting off to the sound of weather slowly erasing the names of the dead.

He's lost his Latin altogether.

He is almost happy.

LUCIFER AT CARDS

In the days before electricity he'd ferret out a game of chance in some saltbox stilted near the ocean. Fishermen playing crib or one-twenties in a kitchen lit by kerosene.

He was a stranger at the door in poor weather. They dealt him in, offered tea and cigarettes, asking after his queer complexion, if his people were from upalong. They didn't have money enough to gamble, wagering their hands with matchsticks. Honour was the only thing at stake.

Hours in the stifling heat of a wood stove, among the endlessly shuffled cards, the mild Shakespearean cursing. He wouldn't remove his hat and they let it be, though he knew it bothered them. He never lost and they were too hospitable to ask him to leave, even after they divined who was sitting at their table.

He admired that. Their conviction that manners trumped all other considerations.

It's mostly internet poker now, or Texas Hold'em with a minimum buy-in, a horseshoe of sullen hipsters under flourescents. *Paying to fuck*, is how he thinks of it. He misses the intimacy of those close kitchens. The almost courtly politeness. The milky, sugared tea.

THE DEVIL'S CURE

A treatment or cure that, in the moment,
might be considered worse than the illness itself.
—Aunt Helen, RN

These, the earliest doctors at work among the fishermen and their few
women, their plague of rickety children—missionaries, megalomaniacs,
drunkards. They appeared once a season aboard a charity vessel. Lancing
boils on stageheads. Hacking at limbs past redemption with handsaws,
applying red-hot pokers to cauterize the stumps. Pulling teeth without
anaesthetic, sweat dripping from their faces into the maw of those awful,
open mouths. They preached hellfire between surgeries or drank with the
locals, trying to scalpel their way into the skirts of some young thing.

Everyone dreaded their diabolical visits. Everyone prayed to see them
swan into the harbour, their hands flashing steel.

DEVIL'S FOOTPRINT

For two centuries he suffered the island's troubling dearth of women. Dances rare as hen's teeth, he could smell them from miles off. He brushed his long black coat, practised a theatrical bow. He was the only stranger on the floor and he monopolized the youngest and prettiest all night. Ruining those innocents with his otherworldly grace, his black licorice breath. They would never marry happily.

He disappeared in the early hours of the morning, leaving the smoking imprint of one cloven hoof on the path. Locals still marvelling at that unmistakeable depression in stone. Bifurcated, about the size and shape of a heart.

The devil's unofficial address in countless misbegotten outports.

Adults give it a wide berth on their way for water or rabbits or berries. Only children are willing to inspect the nefarious location up close, nosing for signs, for confirmation. They don't quite believe the stories yet, though they can feel that infection taking root.

There is no cure.

Not a soul walks past it after dark except on a dare, and never a second time. All night it broadcasts its presence to the surrounding houses, like a beacon. Every sleeper banking toward it in their dreams.

LUCIFER ON GEORGE STREET

The cobbled pavement hobbles his cloven feet. He lurches drunkenly as he navigates the drunken crowds, the bleary racket. He wears a leather coat to his ankles, his sulphur stink muted by the cold drizzle. Two city blocks of bars, but for all its rowdy dissipation the street disappoints him. Most of the shamelessness on display is carnival stupidity, infantile gratification. His mirrored horns are dismissed as costume. A girl in a miniskirt drapes her still-warm underwear from one bony thorn. Shit-faced boys crowd him for selfies, flashing their barnyard tongues at the screen. These are his children, by all accounts. The thought makes him want to eat something raw.

He has always felt more at home in a church.

WHITE DEVIL

A cupful of gasoline suspended in a Glad Kitchen Catcher.

That deadening pendulum tick-tocking around an unheated shed at the sharpest edge of the Labrador sea. The youngsters dipping their faces to huff the mineral fumes as some heavy metal band slashes at the bars of a tinny smartphone speaker.

Looming over the shoulder of that furious party is the land God purportedly gave to Cain before the Book of Genesis was in knee-pants. A host of black-robed lawyers litigating that claim in courtrooms elsewhere.

THE BLACK MAN, OR RED INDIANS' DEVIL

A single rudimentary likeness is all we know of it. A thick figure with a long beard, dressed in a cassock of beaver skin. Its large, angular head perched on the torso like an Easter Island carving. Two lung-shaped pouches sag from either side of the cassock like an old woman's breasts and it holds a tiny blackened hand before its face.

The devil's name was *aich-mud-yim,* according to the girl who made the sketch. This was during her time in the capitol, before she was buried in a churchyard among strangers. The white man beside her inscribing an English appellation when she was done.

She claimed to have seen the devil herself, at the lake where the last handful of her people overwintered. It still wanders among the trees above that shoreline, searching for some lost soul who can speak its name.

The produce section is a minor miracle. Avocados year round, on an island with a sub-arctic climate. Bins bristling with the prickly faces of kiwis, with barbed rows of pineapples. Fresh herbs tucked into individual plastic containers like infants in a hospital nursery. An intermittent mist showering its cold attention on the naked perishables.

He watches locals appraise the offerings, palming the bellies of mangoes and papaya. Affronted by the slightest whiff of corruption: if the baby spinach seems on the verge of wilt, if there are spots on the fruit. They've already forgotten what it is to survive a winter on root vegetables and salt, to think of tinned pears as a treat. It's here he dislikes them most intensely—newly ascended to their tropical kingdom and already of the mind they've earned it somehow. They could just as well be a crowd of mainlanders.

Once he's had his fill of the entitlement in produce, he moves on to the bakery, to the saran-wrapped abattoir of the meat department. Taking his sweet time. The supermarket sits on the grounds of an orphanage bulldozed by public outrage a generation ago. He knows exactly where the worst of those childhoods played out—priests' offices and change rooms, the shadowed dormitories. He reconstructs the hellish layout as he pushes an empty cart along the aisles, walking those hallways in his mind. The mewl of weeping innocents follows after him like the stench of boiled cabbage.

It beggars belief to think he is alone with that poisonous soundtrack. But no one else can hear it over the brassy glare of plenty.

DEVILSKIN

...mischievous, prankish boy or man.
—Dictionary of Newfoundland English

We're soldiers now, we crowd. Baker's dozen. Lucky thirteen. The faces on us filled with something like dread, but it's only the camera we're fearful of. Holding right still, as we was ordered.

Come from across the island to sign on and they marched us into a Water Street studio to have our likeness drawn off, before we goes overseas. Fighting the Germans in France. A lark, we figures. Home by Christmas, with stories to tell. It's the notion of a picture's permanence makes us look uncertain of ourselves now. Not wanting to seem foolish in a moment that will be around years after we're dead and gone.

Outfitted in our uniforms, buttoned to the throat and bagging at the waist and the knees, like hand-me-downs from an army of older brothers. As if they expects we'll grow into them once the fighting starts. No insignia, nor medals, nor weapons. Balaclavas perched high on our heads and tipped left or right to look worldly, to look carefree. *Devilskin* is what we thinks, *hard tickets*. Not seeing how the hats makes us seem more like the boys we're trying not to be. A sombre squad of elves, hardly a one of us old enough to shave.

The back row standing at attention and then a handful in chairs. The smallest two among us cross-legged on the floor. One reaching up to hold hands with the soldier sot behind him. To say how they are friends. That's how much we knows about France now, that is. That's what we knows about war.

A pair of woollen trigger mitts alongside the second youngster out front. The kind we wears hunting a feed of turr in the spring, the index finger free so's we can fire a rifle. Putting those poor creatures to wing from their nests and picking them off, one by one.

It's knowing what's to become of us makes you crowd pause over them mitts. Makes them seem an ill omen. So pale in the margins of the frame it's a job to make them out. It could be any one of us laid them there as we filed to our places and turned to face the camera. Waited for the flash.

Knit by someone's mother, they was.

THE HINGES

He's always had a soft spot for mothers. Their prodigal faithfulness, their capacity for suffering. Every graveyard on the island pocked with pint-sized headstones, angelic sheep carved into their marble brows. And the mothers carry on setting their bread to rise and scrubbing their scabby hands raw in laundry tubs. Picking nits from the heads of the pisswigs not yet taken by tuberculosis or chin-cough or scarlet fever, by dropsy or the bloody flux, the nine-day-fits. By drowning. The door between this world and the next swinging wide on a mother's labours, her thankless torment. Arms trembling with the effort of carting her ineffable losses to and from the back garden, the brook, the flakes on the landwash.

He can only marvel at the ghoulish engineering that keeps the architecture from collapse. It makes him feel like a dilettante. Even the women who sour as they age make their beet salads and trifles for church suppers, they still kneel at their bedsides to ask a blessing on the quick and the dead.

Winter nights they stand on the front bridge in their small clothes, passing through the mortifications of *the change*. Their modesty stripped away by spells of feverish heat, of groundless dread. Steam moldering from their foreheads in the cold. *I'm as hot as the hinges of hell*, they mutter to the darkness. As if they know he is close enough to hear.

SAVIOUR'S LETTER

A letter, usu printed, purporting to be by Christ,
kept as a moral guide and as a charm.
—Dictionary of Newfoundland English

He used to peddle the letter door-to-door, just for badness. Reading it aloud to the illiterate in their mean kitchens, preaching its virtues to steal the bit of cash money they'd squirrelled away in a jar, in a sock under a floorboard. Written by Christ Himself, he told them. Safe delivery in child-bed to the bearer. Freedom from bodily hurt. A spell against fire and barbarous weather and the Dark One himself. It was like an angel kept tame in a drawer to protect the house and all within. Some gave every cent they had to purchase a second copy for the fishing boat.

Easy marks, the crowd of them. Born naked and knowing how quickly they might be stripped bare again. It gave him a little quiver of pleasure to see them trace the mysterious letters with a finger, as if they could hear the Lord speaking through their skin. He'd written the thing himself during one of the old European plagues, waking to a vicious hangover and wanting to share the misery. He might still be selling them if he hadn't tired of the locals' credulousness. Of making them feel less alone in the world, however briefly.

LUCIFER AT HEALTH SCIENCES EMERG

When the moon is full he visits the emergency department. Arriving early to take the same corner seat in the waiting room, basking in the roil of lunacy and torment. As if it was a garden on a bright afternoon, the sun's heat simmering balm from the flower beds.

The room has the oppressive feel of a crowded train crossing the Gobi Desert. Stalled on the rails hours at a time, the same featureless view to the horizon, the overflow standing in the aisles or seated on the filthy floor. The indignant picking their way through the congestion to confront the conductor seated behind glass, demanding an explanation for the delay.

There is no explanation. The moon is full.

Without fail, some drunk with an ugly gash in his forehead will make a scene, screaming as he strips off his clothes or tries to kill an underpaid security guard before the police are summoned to wrestle him out the door. After that jolt of motion, the room settles back into the claustrophobic stasis of internment. People clutching their individual agonies like lottery tickets as the seconds tick over. Each passing moment adding credence to the belief their name will never be called.

It's enough to carry him through the month ahead, watching that conviction stamp across their features like the price of groceries ringing up on an old-fashioned cash register.

His namesake, once upon a time: Devil's Cove, a reference to the job it was climbing off the beach, dragging their fish and gear and jelly legs up that hellish incline. He was almost touched by it. As if they had marked their doorways with lamb's blood to request he pass over, leave their dwellings be. Until some dough-headed clergyman began preaching against the demonic moniker. Insisting the town publish letters in the St. John's papers to announce a rechristening, to clarify their spiritual allegiances.

    Job's Cove is what they settled on.

    Poor righteous blameless Job. It was impossible not to hate the man, seeing him happy after all the apocalyptic suffering. Accepting the latest crop of wives and children as fair compensation for his lost wives and children. Giving thanks for the newly fecund cattle. For the innocent goats in the field.

LUCIFER AT ST. PAT'S MERCY HOME

sin n *OED* ~ 3 a (c1300–1470), still in colloq use.
A cause for regret, 'a shame,' usu said in reproach
for a cruel or thoughtless deed
          —Dictionary of Newfoundland English

The home is on his rounds but there are days he can't face the spectacle of
geriatrics being spoon-fed in their wheelchairs. Losing the names and faces
of their children under sofa cushions in the visitors' lounge. Pissing
themselves raw. Not a soul here has the barest notion who he is. If he isn't
mistaken for a long-dead father or one of their misplaced youngsters, the
bovine faces stare blankly from their beds, without anticipation or fear.
Settling into ruin like the derelict outport houses featured so often in
tourist photos, in what passes for poetry in the little magazines. Roofs
caving and glass gone from the window frames. The weather getting in.

That sort of tripe.

A sin, is how the locals speak of it—a sin the state these folks have fallen
into. Meaning something altogether different from what the word should
signify. Invariably, he leaves feeling sorry for himself. Not one of those
fading creatures was worth the effort he put into seeding their days with
misery and despair. It makes him think being here may have been a waste of
his time, of his singular talents.

TRANSIENT

He loved riding the trains, back when there were trains. The Newfie Bullet making its soporific trek across the island's interior, a blinkered mule on rails. Passengers stupefied by the trudge, by the endless iterations of bog and scrub crawling past the windows. His captive congregation. Even the strictest Methodists entertained his sooty overtures when snow stalled them for days on the Gaff Topsails. Bored to temptation, desperate for the relief of fresh company.

The children of Adam believe in the soul as they believe in the weather: a fickle, shifting thing. Something transient. Heaven and hell cross their horizon like clouds driven by the wind, neither substantial enough to hold a grapple. He used to think this was their great weakness, but he's given up the certainty.

He walks the narrow rail-bed now the trains are gone, the ties pulled like rotting teeth. A fixture on the trail, pilgrim in a ragged overcoat, his infernal stench like a lingering pall of creosote. For years his only encounters were with passing mountain bikes and quads, with standoffish moose and black bear. But lately he's noticed coyotes eyeing him from the bush—the most recent island stowaways, newly arrived on sea ice floating down from Labrador and still assessing the unfamiliar territory. Trying to decide if he is predator or prey. Whether he might be fit to eat.

A DEPARTURE   11/04/2019

There you are now. The lost child.
In an empty departure lounge without luggage
or companions, your cell phone disabled.

A boarding pass that promises a seat
will be assigned at the gate,
a stoner's budding apprehension on the verge

of something shapeless and absolute.
The high ceilings and ceramic tile
echoing every generic turnstile

you've passed through: Pearson. Dallas/Fort Worth.
Helsinki, en route to a gold camp north
of the Arctic Circle—such a fairy-tale

sheen to that image the ancient Norse
might have employed it as a likeness
for radiant Valhalla. But your work in the field

was a keelhaul through the tamer regions
of some medieval underworld,
staking and trenching while insect legions

boiled the air around your head or, shackled
to a hammer, breaking rock like a prisoner
sentenced to purgatorial labour.

It nearly broke you, child of leisure,
of millennial luxury. Twice you tried to quit
before setting your shoulder to that adult freight,

shrugging off its routine torment
with the obscenities you'd mastered in Finnish,
signing on for a second stint

as the summer's tour tapered through August.
Near the end of your brief, unguarded residence
on the earth. Beloved. Blessed.

By now you've twigged to the strange quiet
about the terminal: a stillness in the absence
of other passengers, a stark Northern light

slanting across the deserted chairs
that recalls your time in the Lapland forests.
Those lean Arctic days. The numberless stars.

You've almost put a finger on it
when your name comes over the public address.
Then the same stranger's voice is calling your flight.

ACKNOWLEDGEMENTS

The longer I'm at this racket, the more I appreciate what a privilege it is to be closely read. Kevin Connolly was the good shepherd for this book at Anansi as well as its meticulous and generous editor. Stan Dragland and Gary Draper both took a run at earlier versions of the manuscript, out of the goodness of their hearts. Gil Adamson signed on as a copy-editor, but I'm grateful she didn't let that title limit her influence on the book. My thanks to all of them for their invaluable attention.

Thanks to Sarah MacLachlan for reaching out in the early days of the pandemic and asking to see this manuscript.

The poems in "You Are Here" felt like a private project for most of the decade I've been working on them, a way to look at a familiar world through a different lens. Hopefully there's something in them worth sharing. Most of the little I know about Tomas Tranströmer and his work comes from the following collections:

Windows and Stones, translated by May Swenson with Leif Sjöberg.
Selected Poems, edited by Robert Haas.
For the Living and the Dead: Poems and a Memoir.
Bright Scythe, translated by Patty Crane.

My apologies to Tranströmer and his translators for the liberties taken, and the missteps, lapses, and failings I am undoubtedly guilty of in this solemn and absurd undertaking.

Alysia Shewchuk created the beautiful book design. The maps included in "You Are Here" and "The Dark Woods" were put together by Arielle Hogan.

The illustration at the beginning of "Devilskin" is a detail from *Canada orientale nell'America settentrionale* by Vincenzo Coronelli (1650-1718), available online through the Centre for Newfoundland Studies at Memorial University. The full map can be found at https://collections. mun.ca/digital/collection/maps/id/205/rec/92.

Thanks to Elisabeth Gießauf for her help and hospitality in Austria. To Zuzana Janouskova for the visit to the Punkva Caves in the Czech Republic. Thanks to Michal and Magda Alenowicz and Tomek Krupa for looking after me and my daughter Robin during our travels in Poland, and to Michal for the parting gifts of Zbignew Herbert and Adam Zagajevski.

Most of all, I'm grateful to my wife Holly for holding the ship steady these last few years. My thanks to her, and to Arielle and Robin and Mike, for helping keep Ben close.

Michael Crummey

MICHAEL CRUMMEY is the author of twelve books of poetry and fiction. He was the inaugural winner of the $50,000 Writers' Trust Fellowship in recognition of "exceptional creative ability and outstanding promise" in his work to date. His most recent novel, *The Innocents*, won the Thomas Raddall Atlantic Fiction Award and was a finalist for the Scotiabank Giller Prize, the Governor General's Literary Award, and the Rogers Writers' Trust Fiction Prize. *Little Dogs: New and Selected Poems* appeared in 2017. He lives in St. John's, where he is starting to feel his age.